This Comic Book Belongs to:

Are you enjoying this awesome book?

If so, please leave a review because we would love to hear about your creative stories, amazing artwork, and silly characters! We use your feedback to create even better books for you to enjoy in the future.

Thank you so much. You are amazing!

SMART KIDS PRINTING PRESS

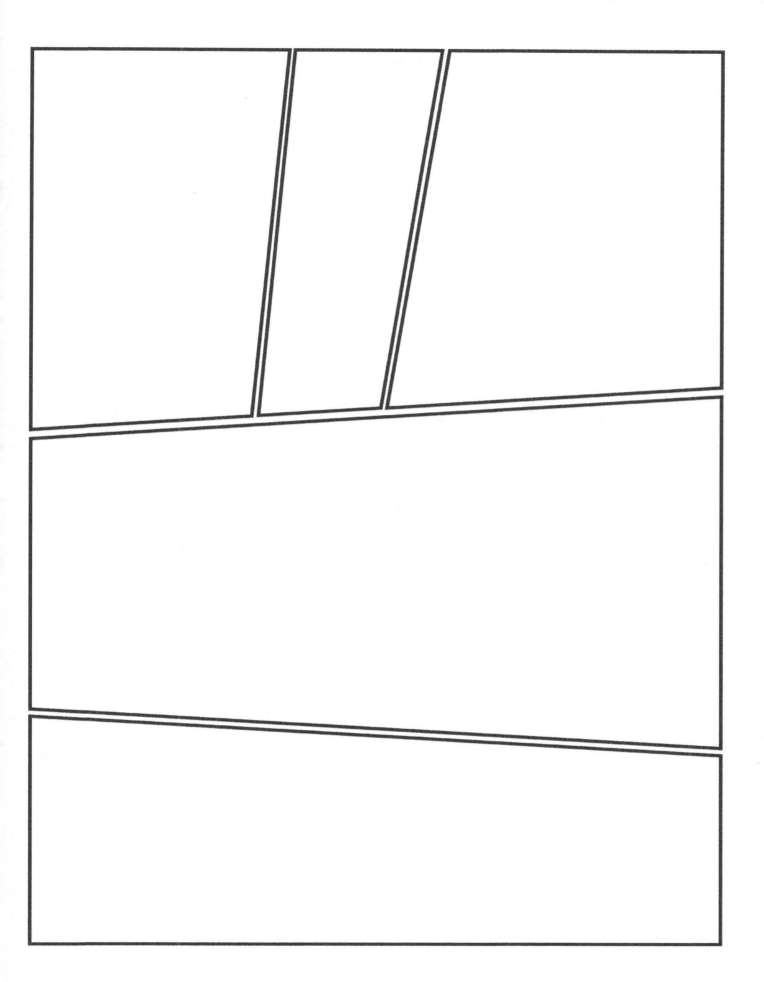

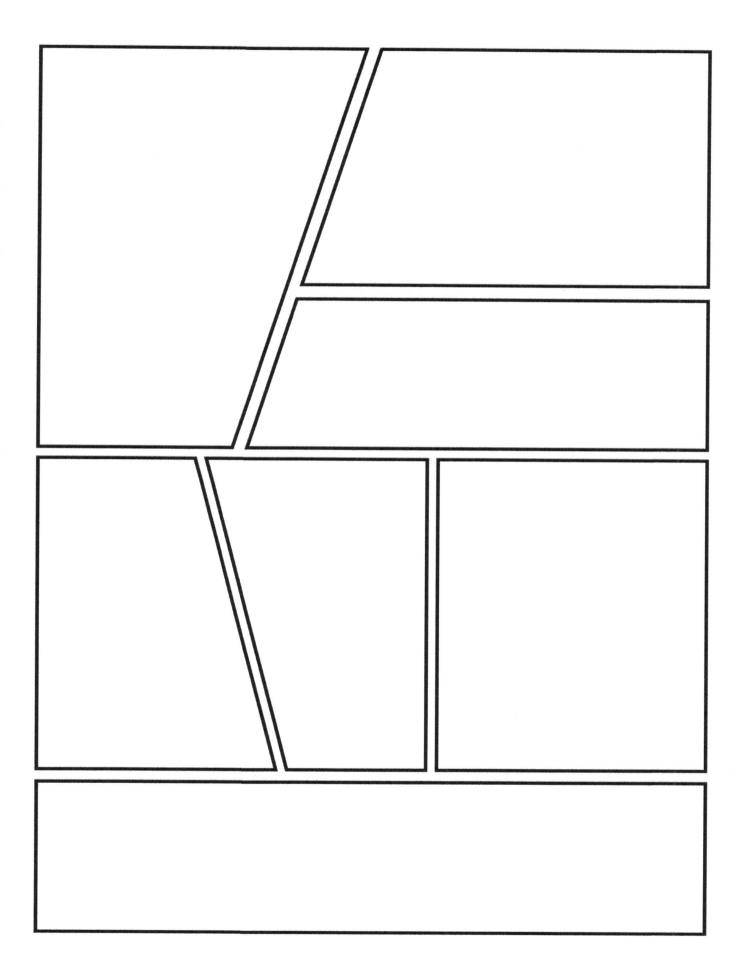

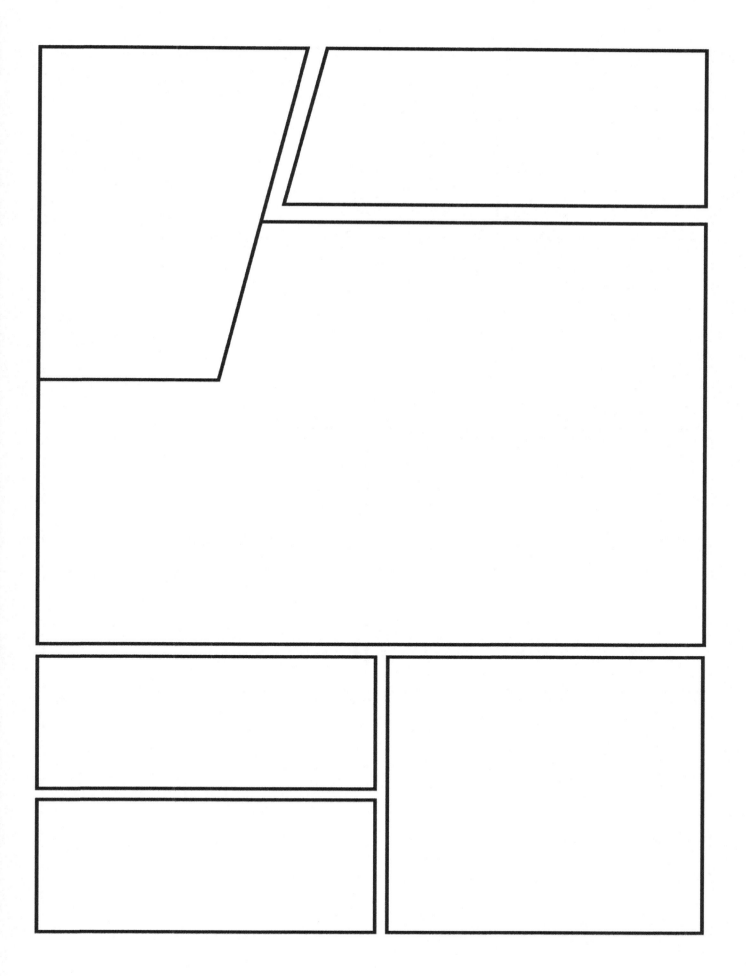

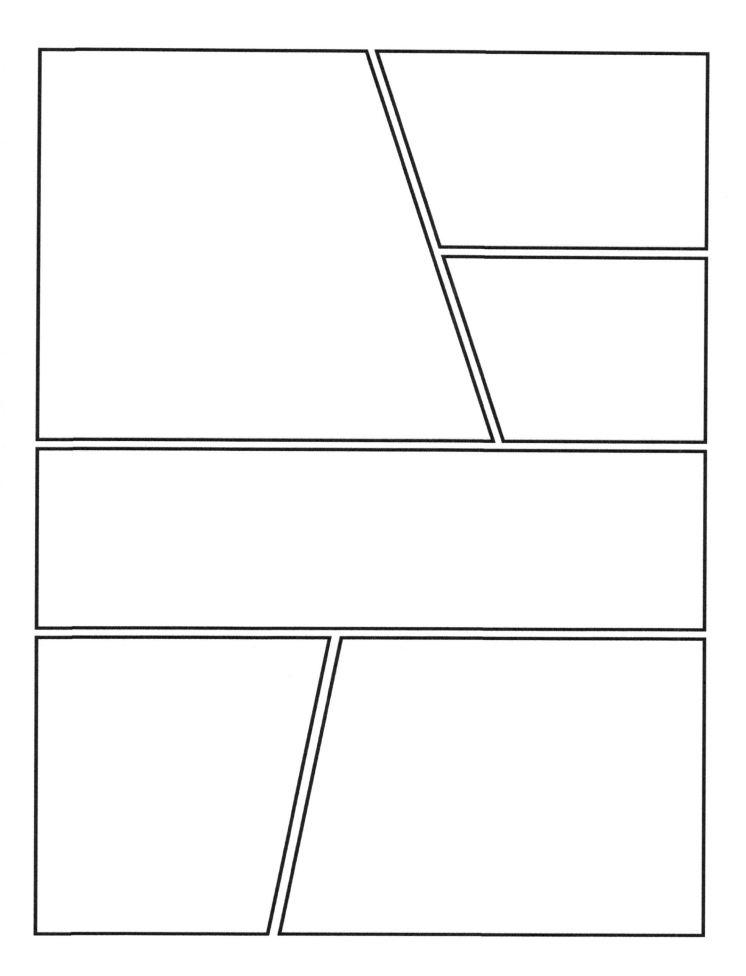

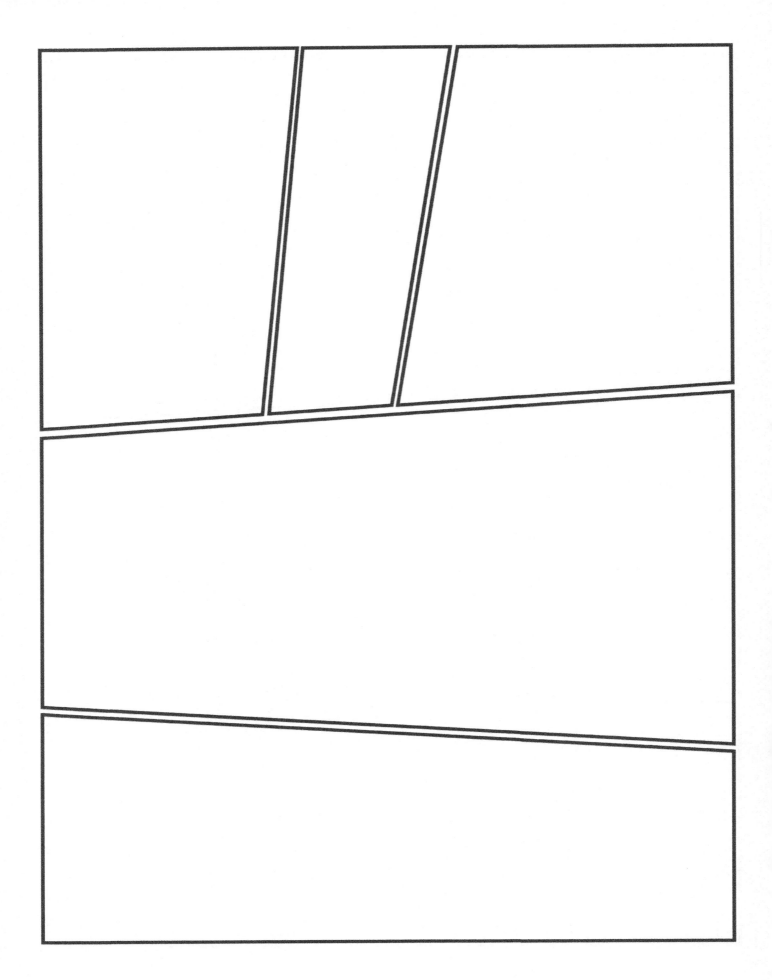

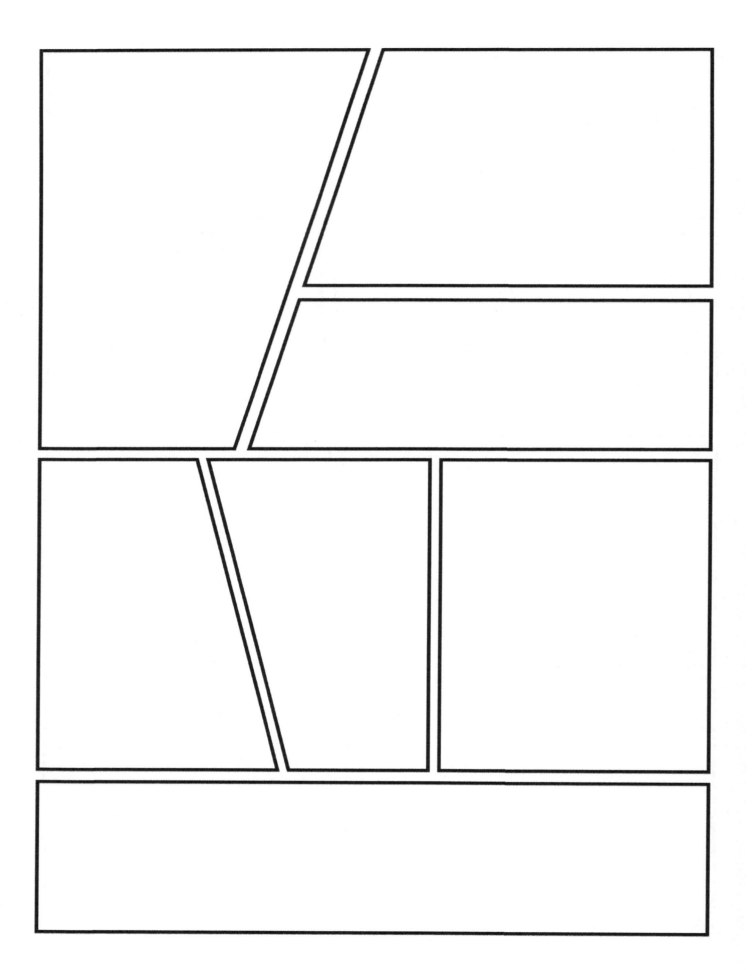

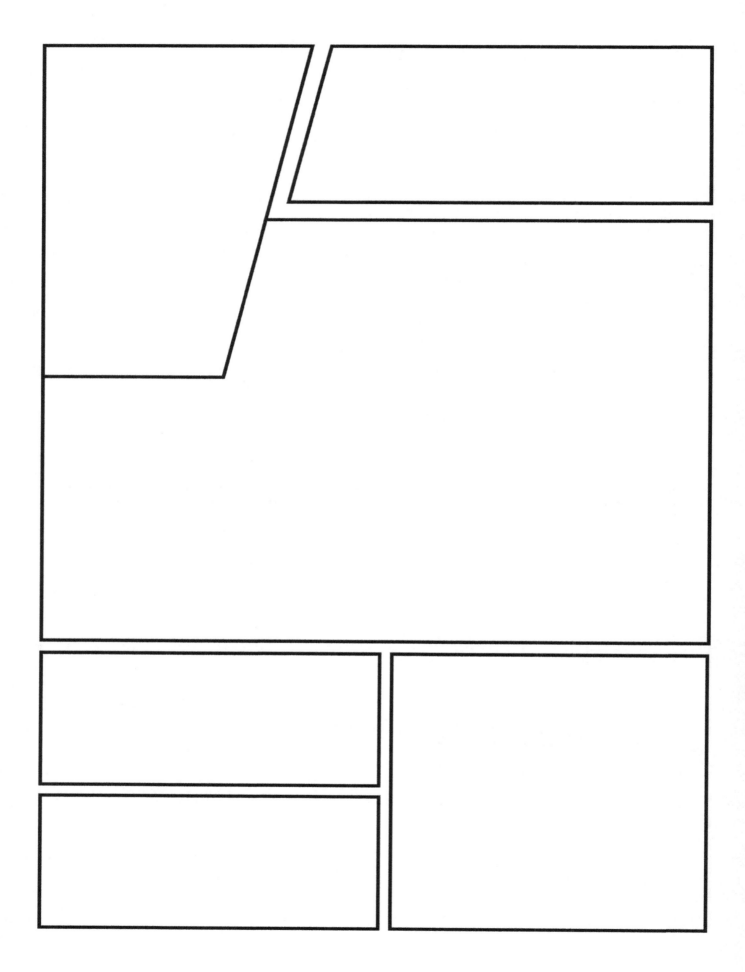

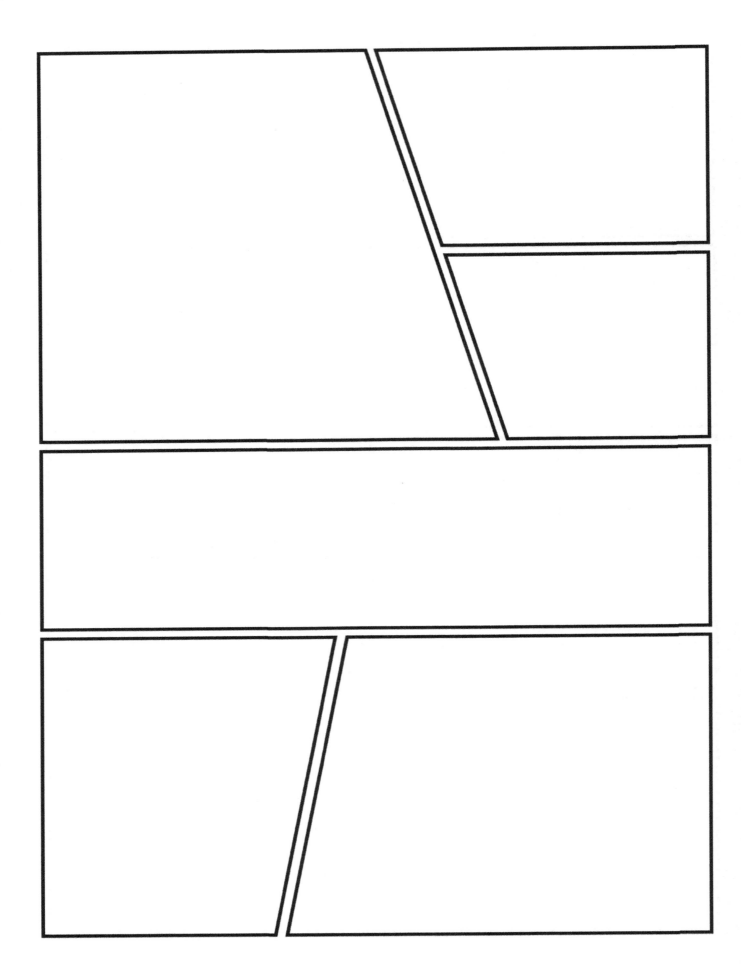

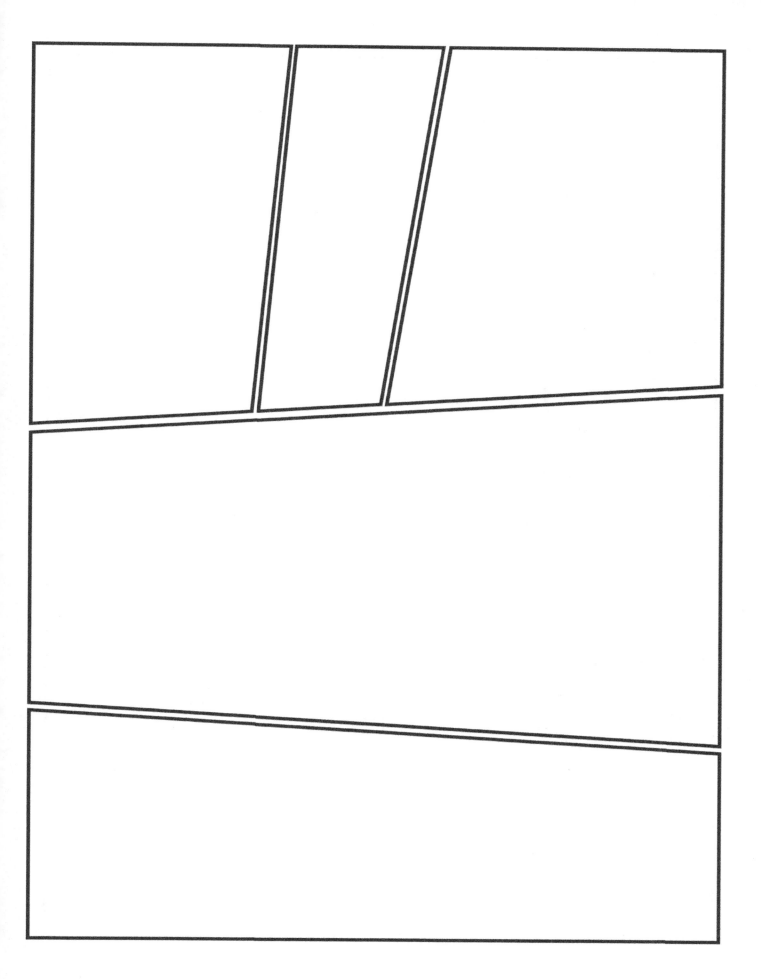

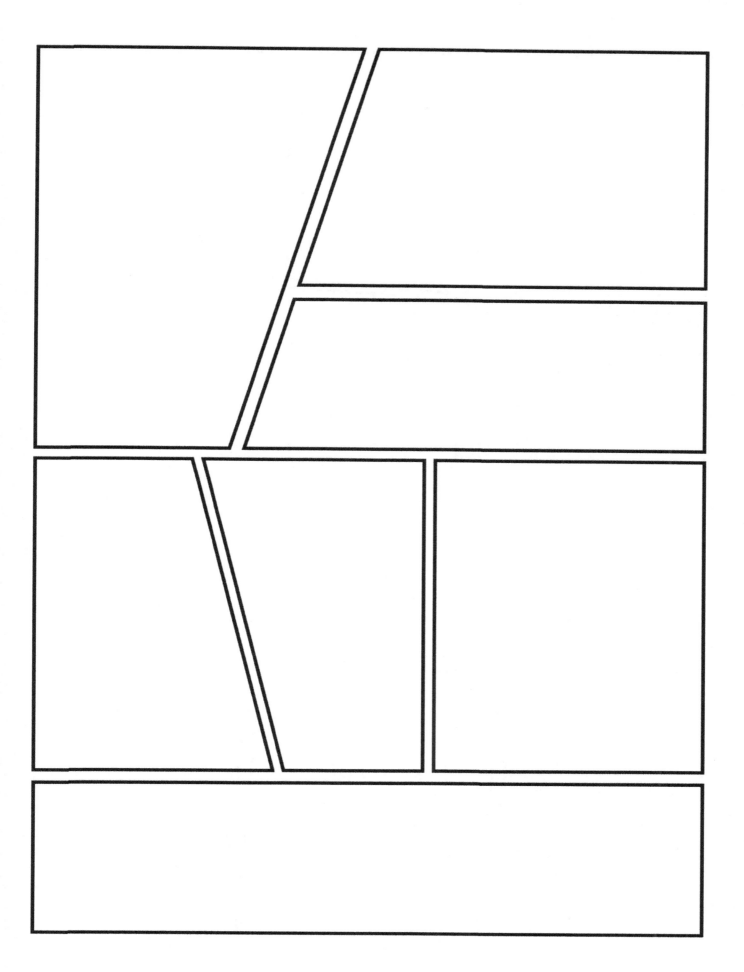

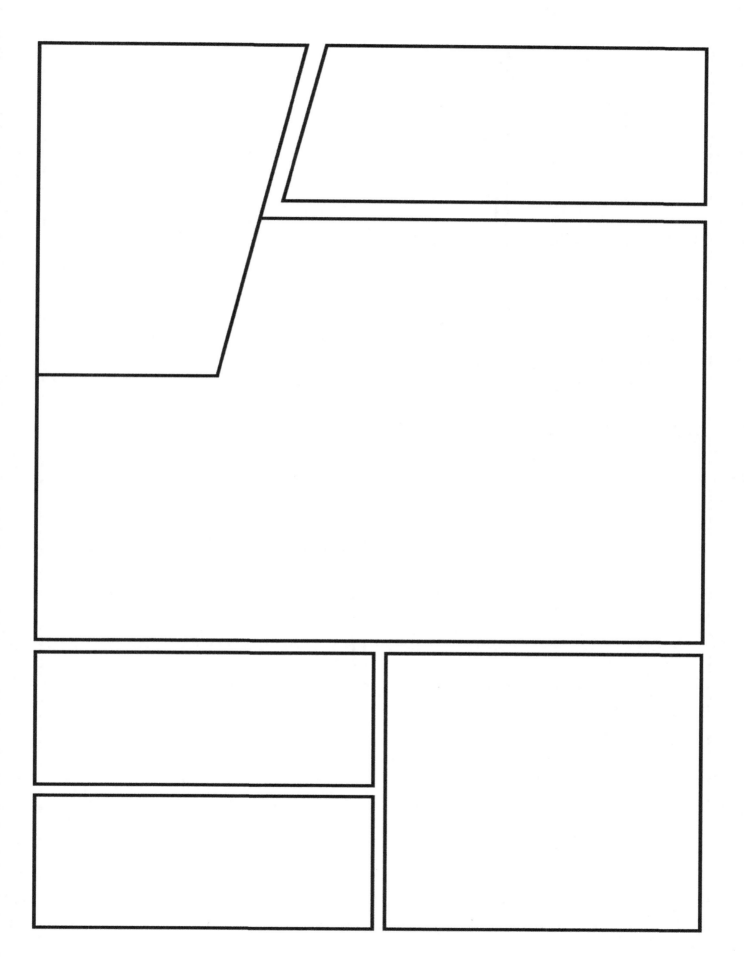

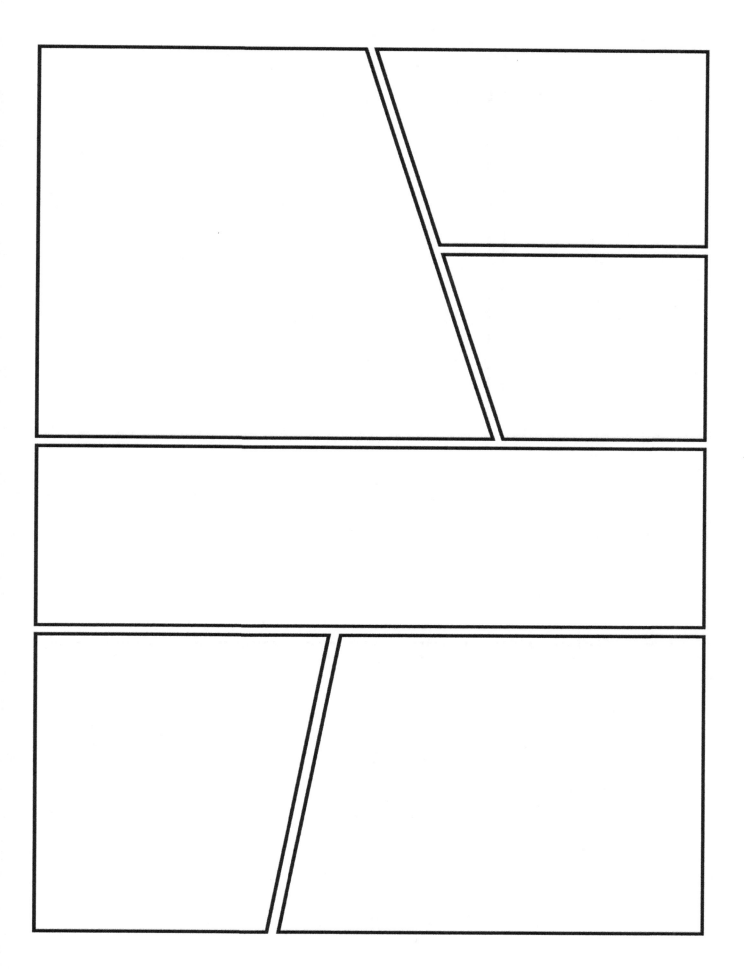

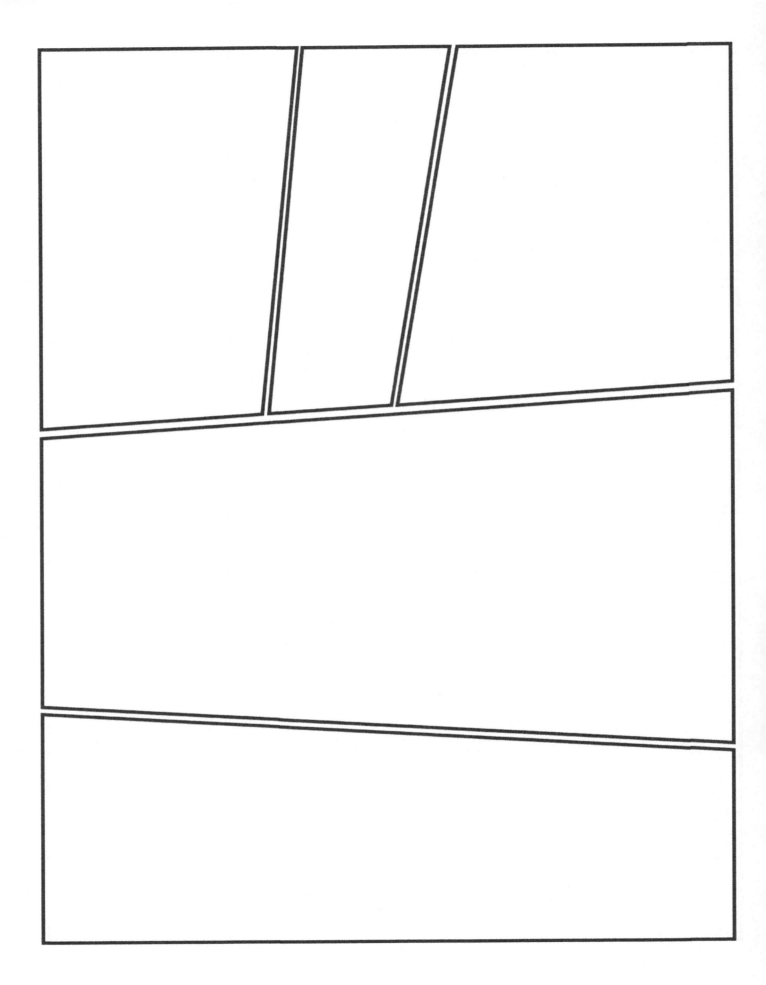

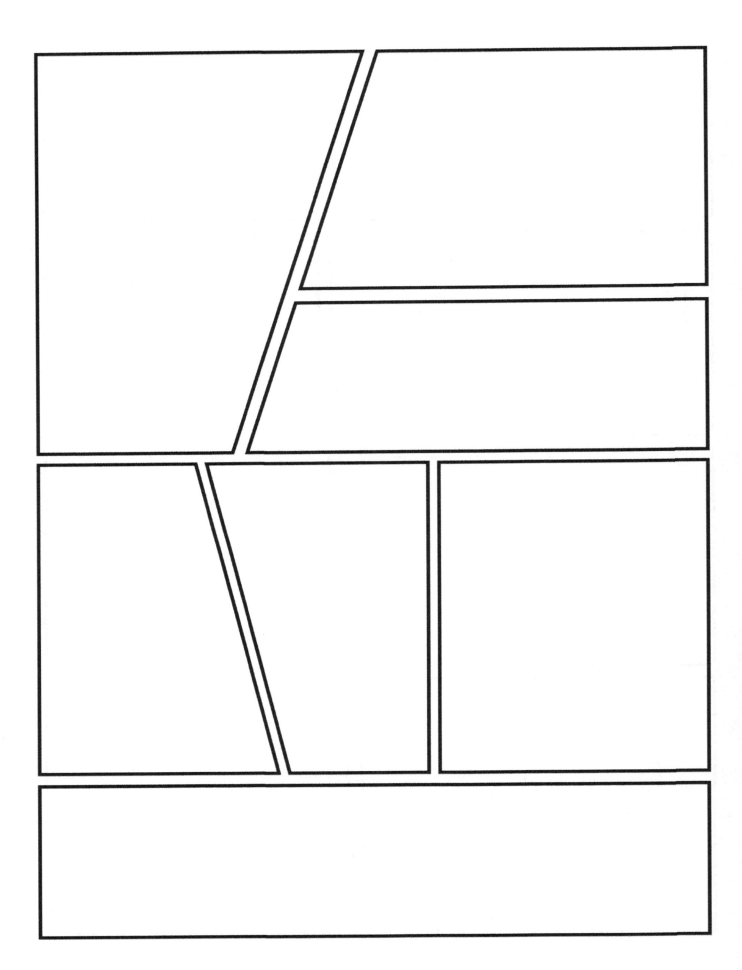

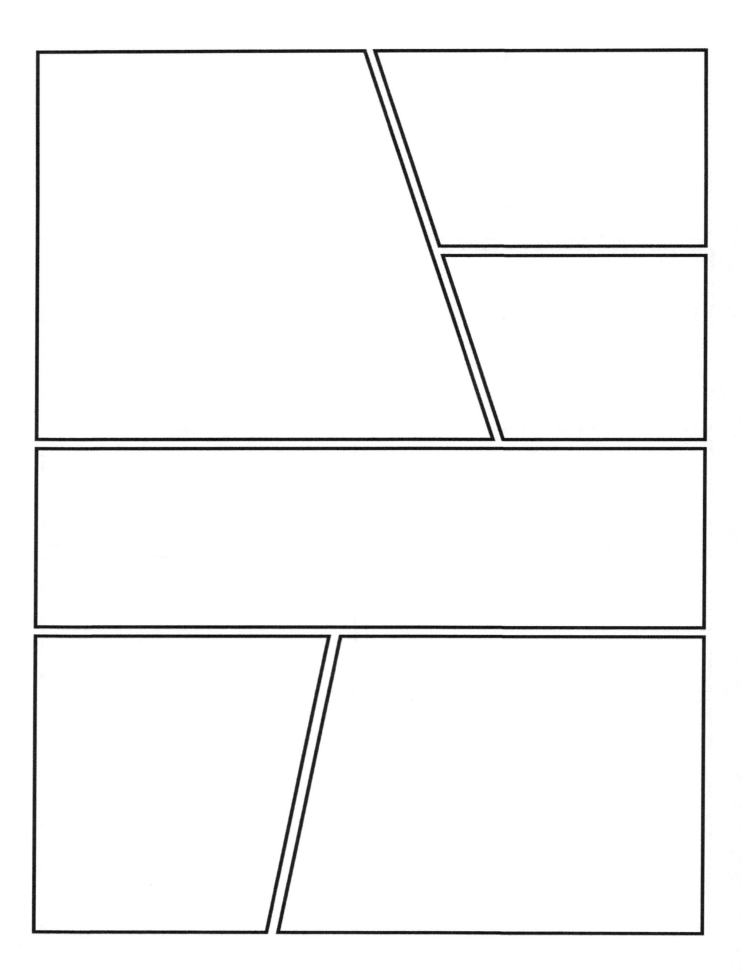

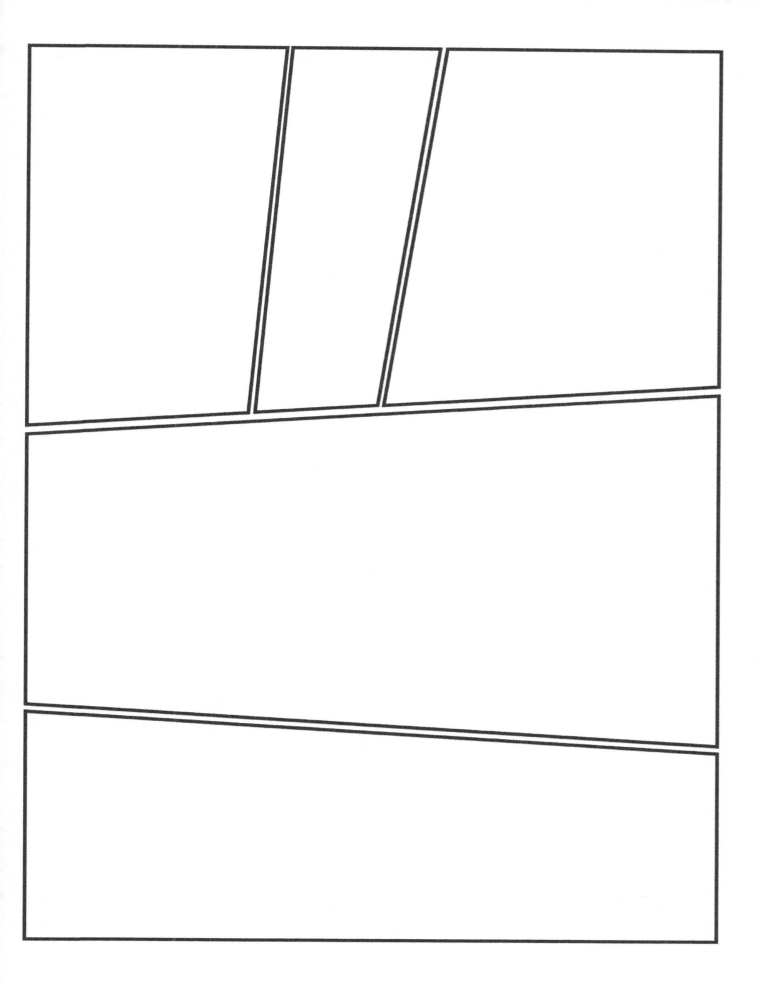

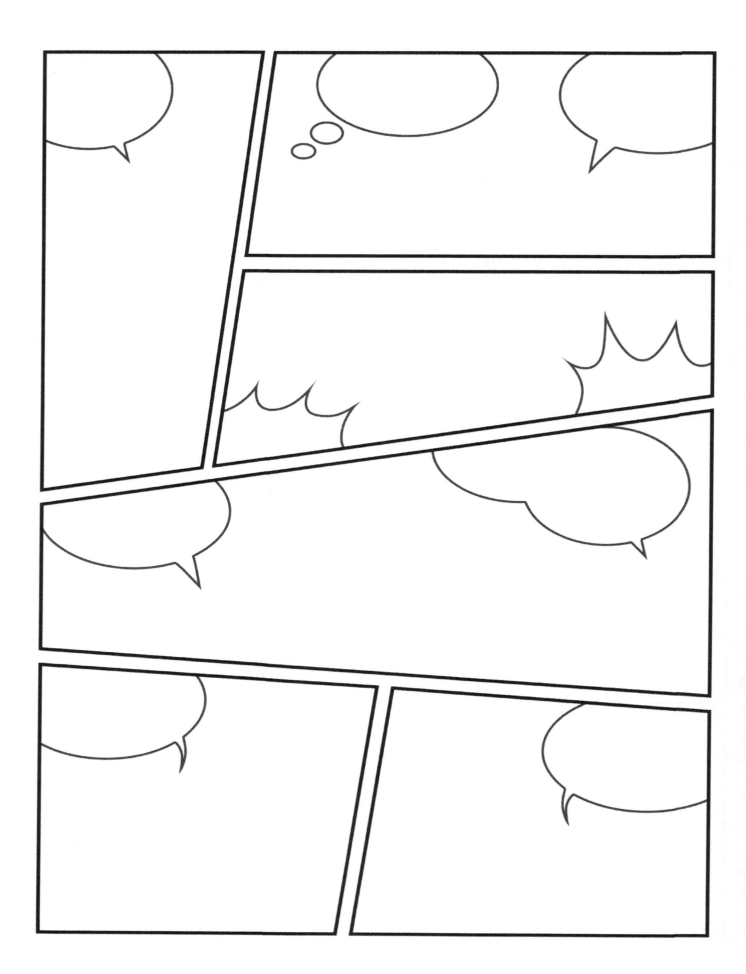

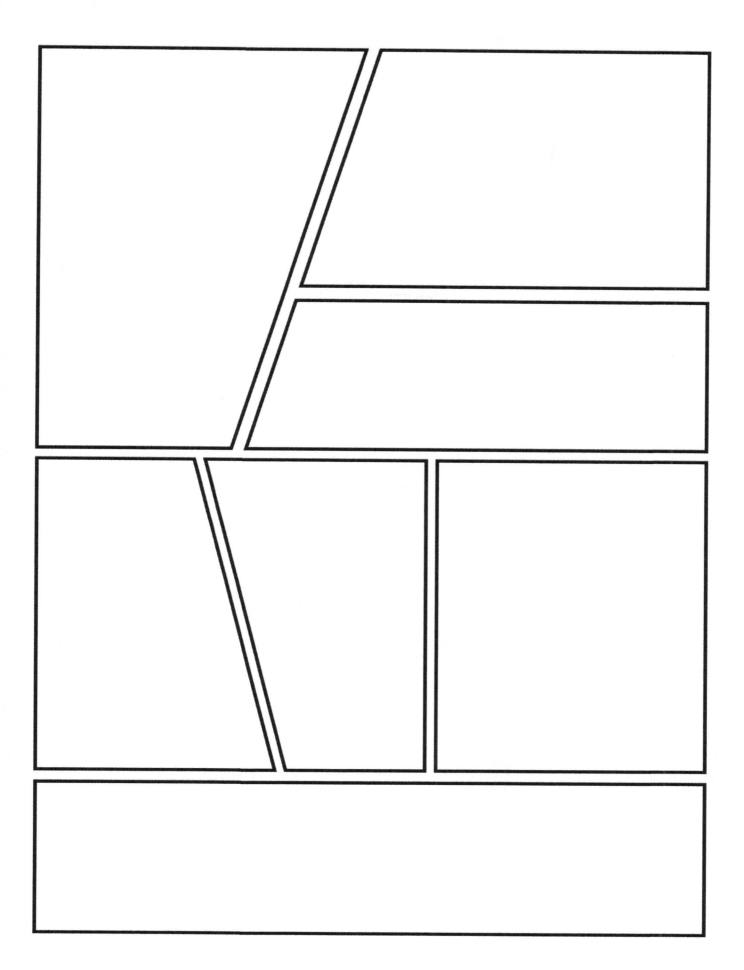

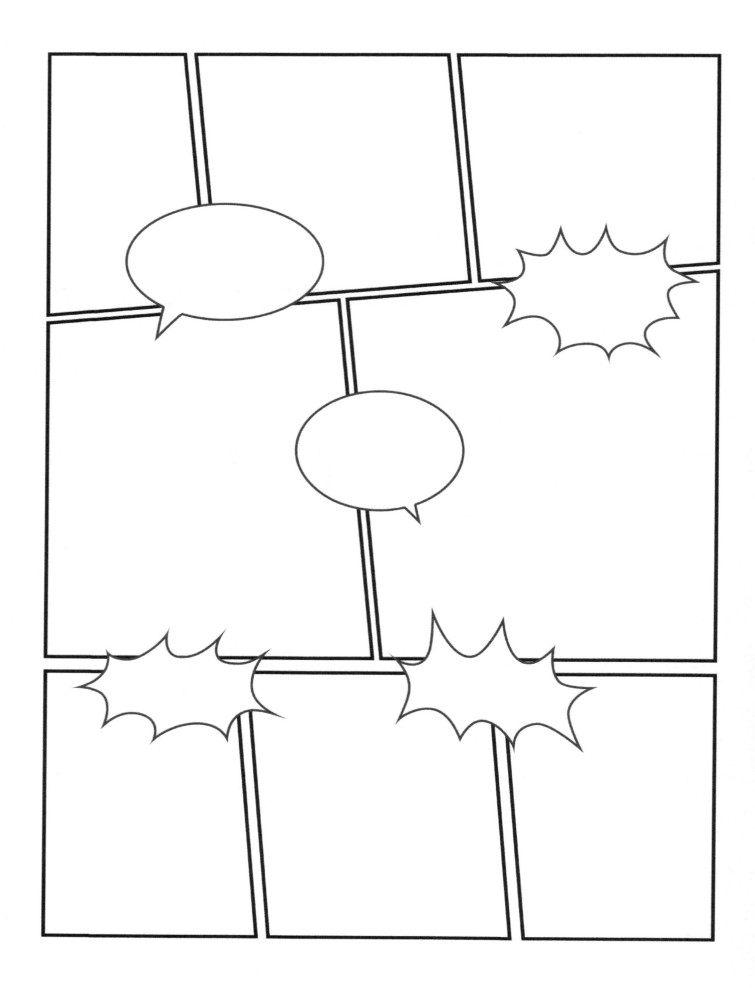

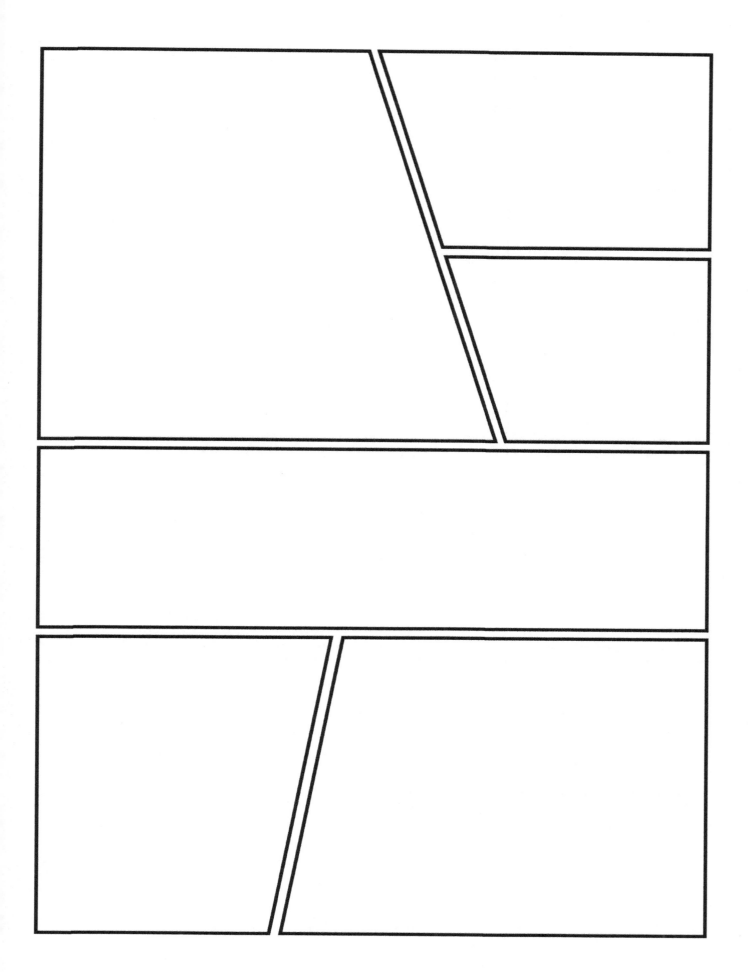

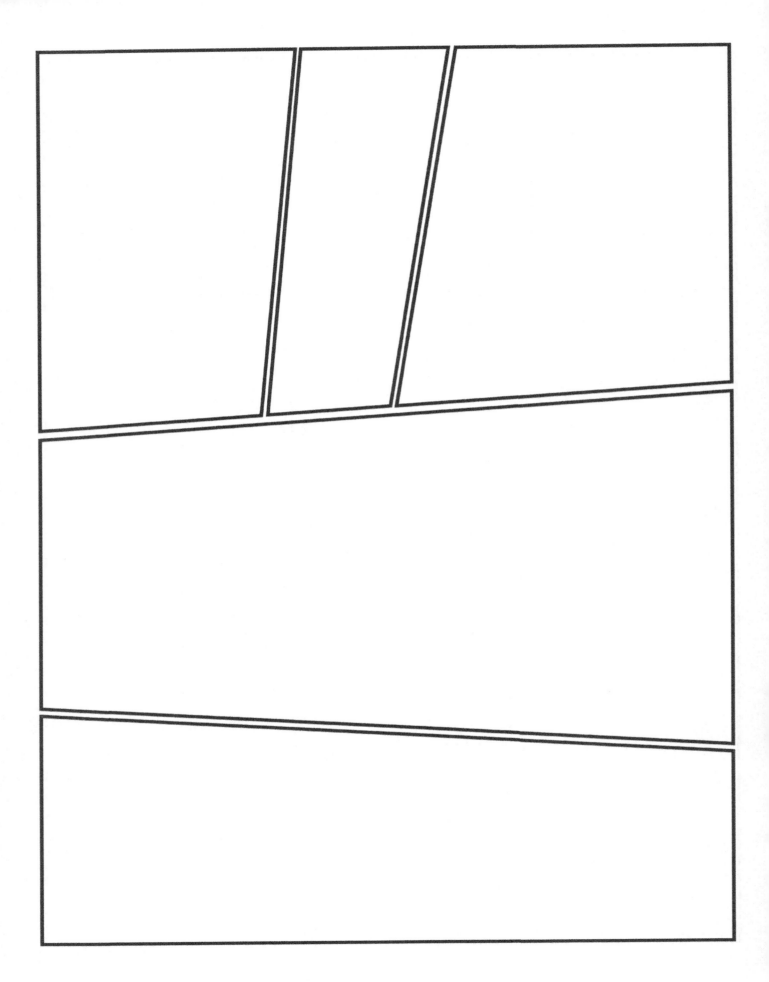

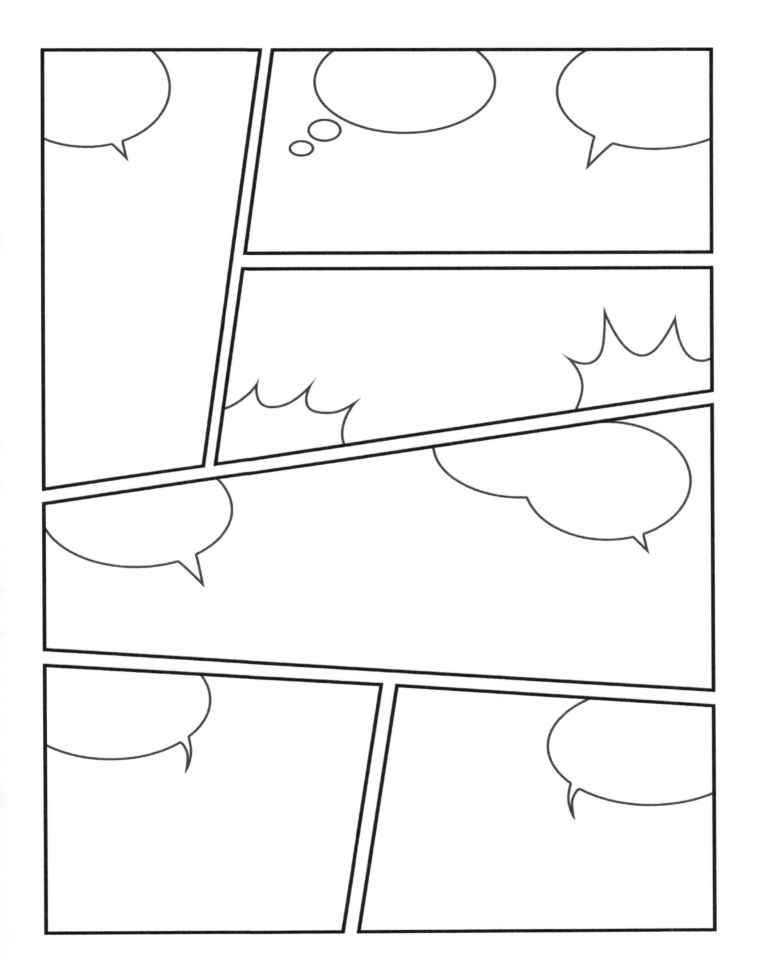

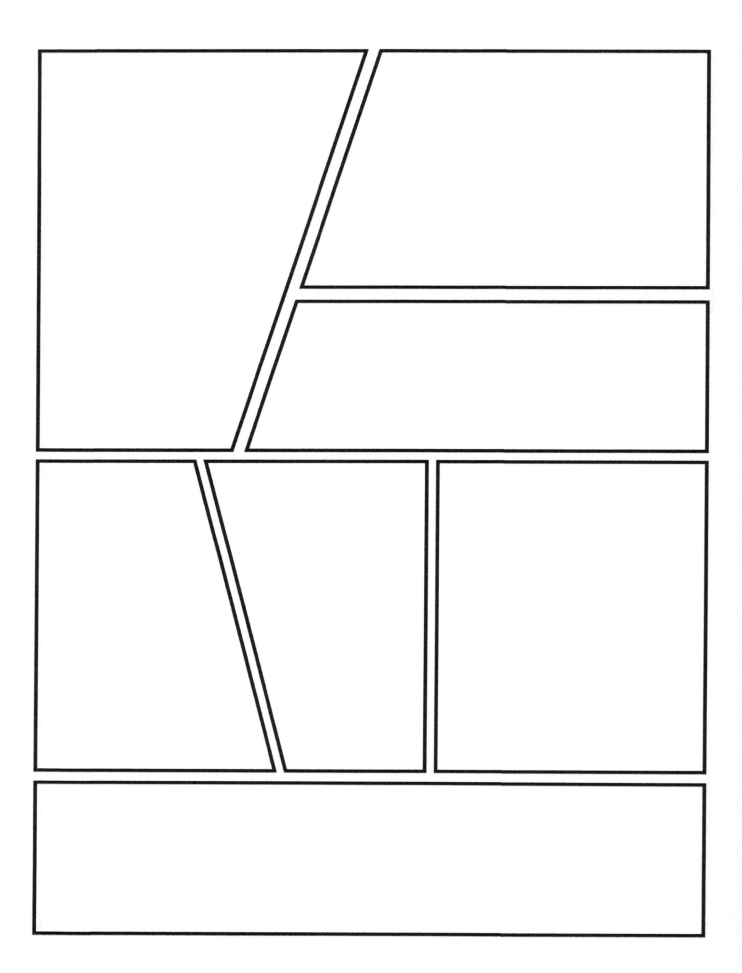

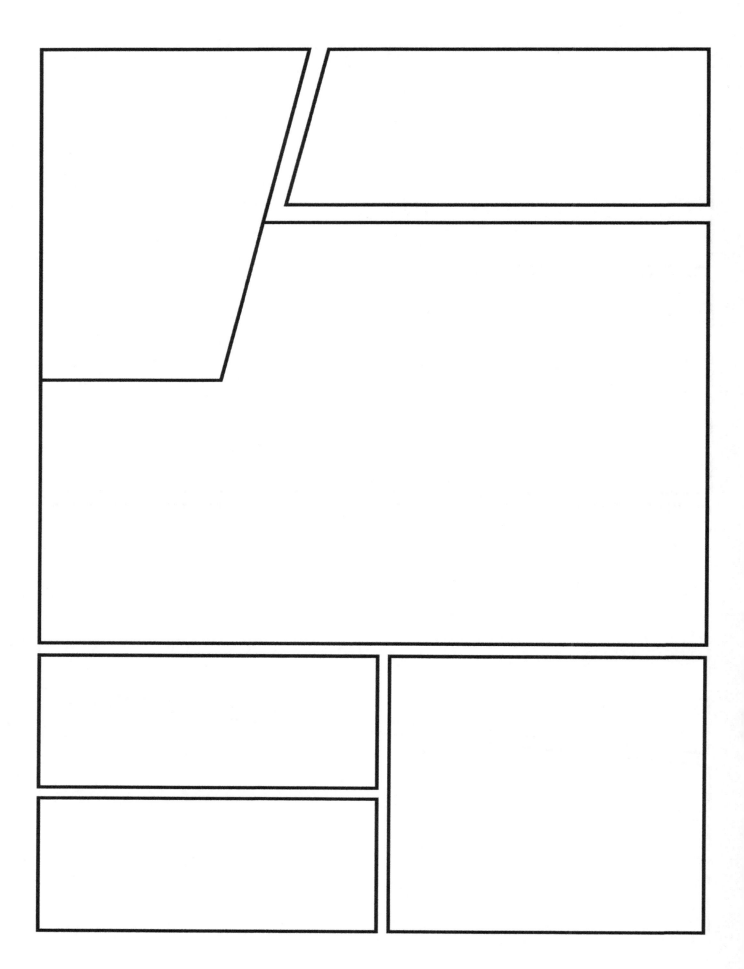

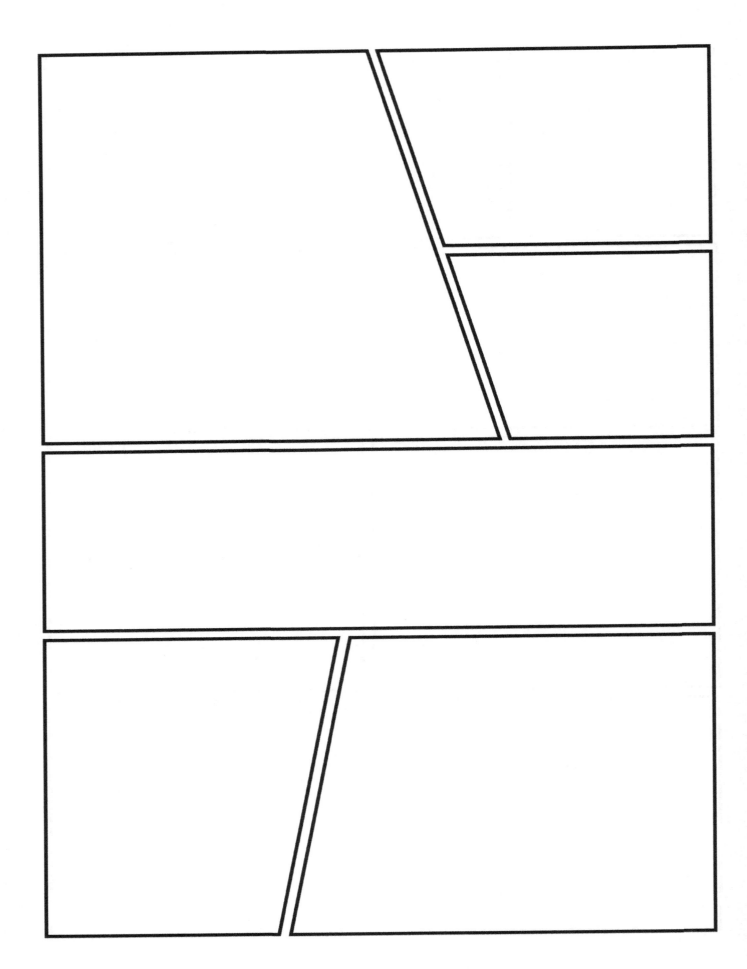

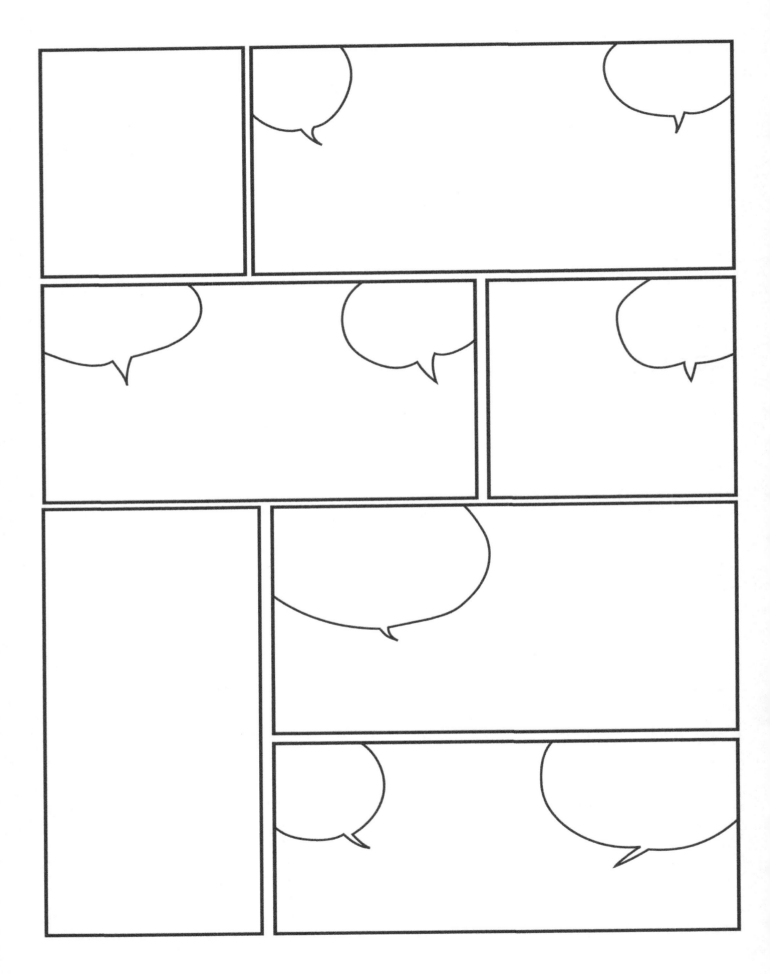

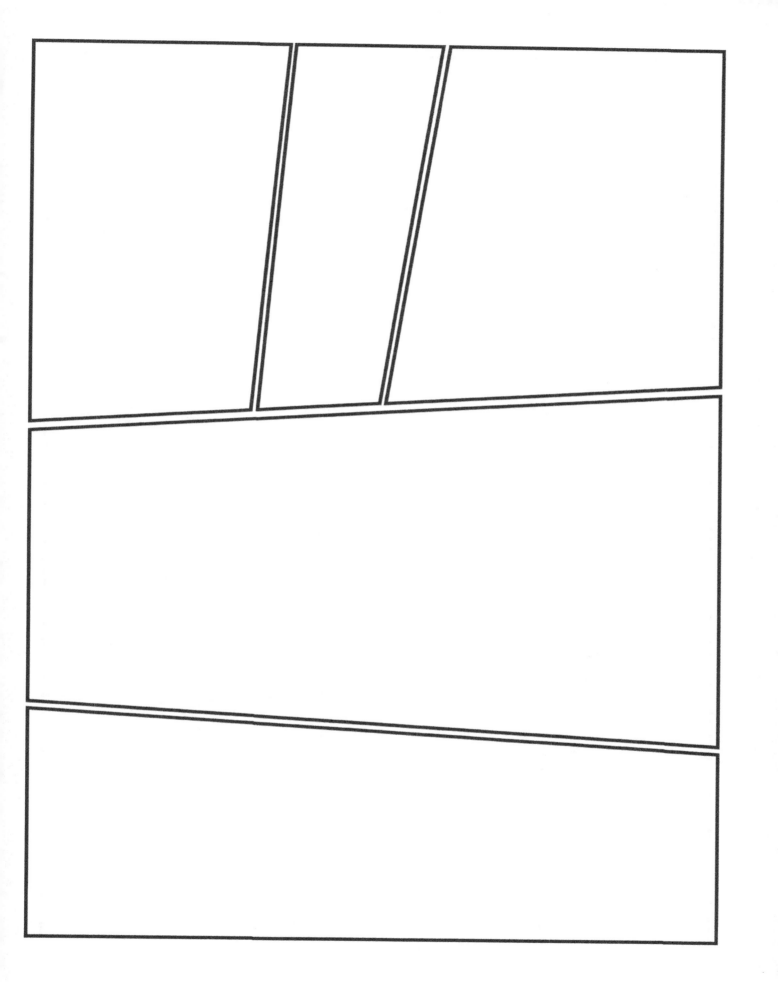

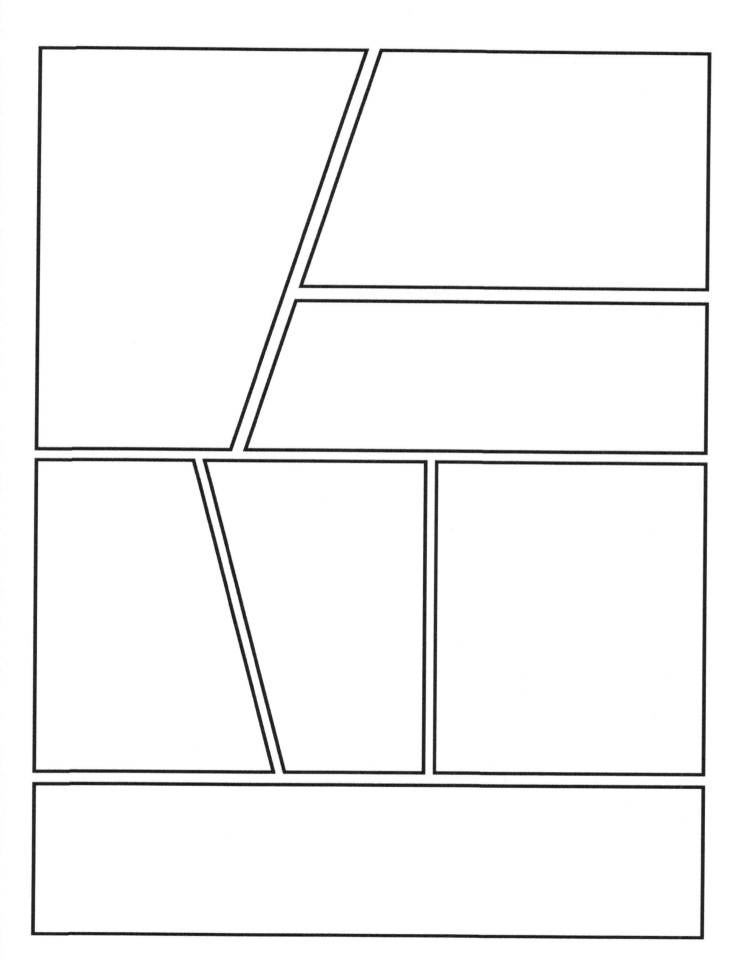

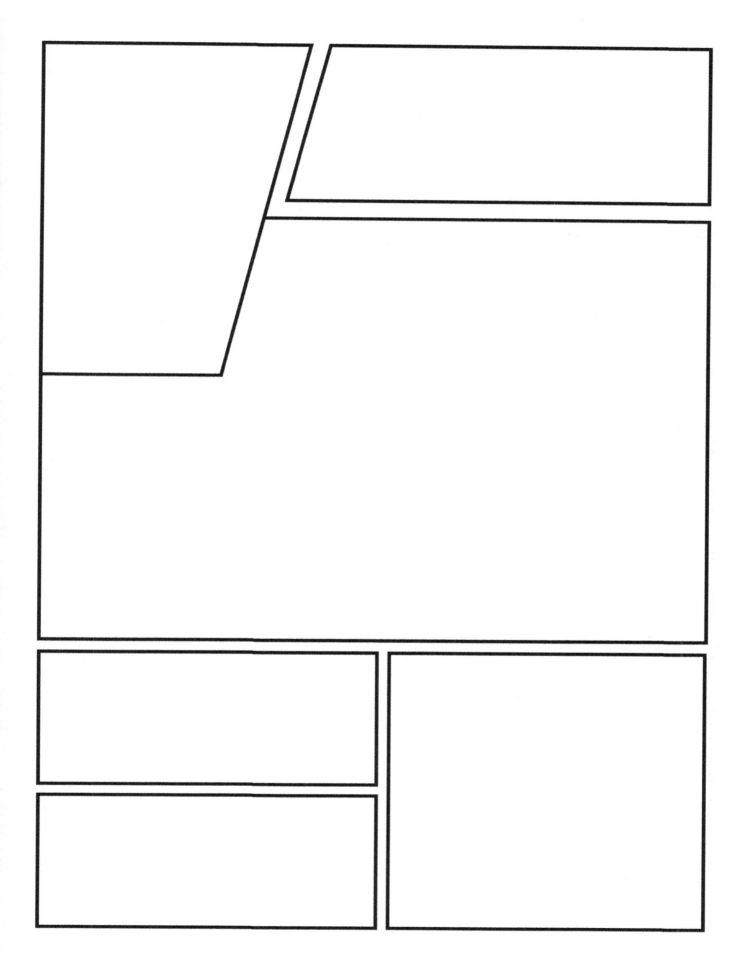

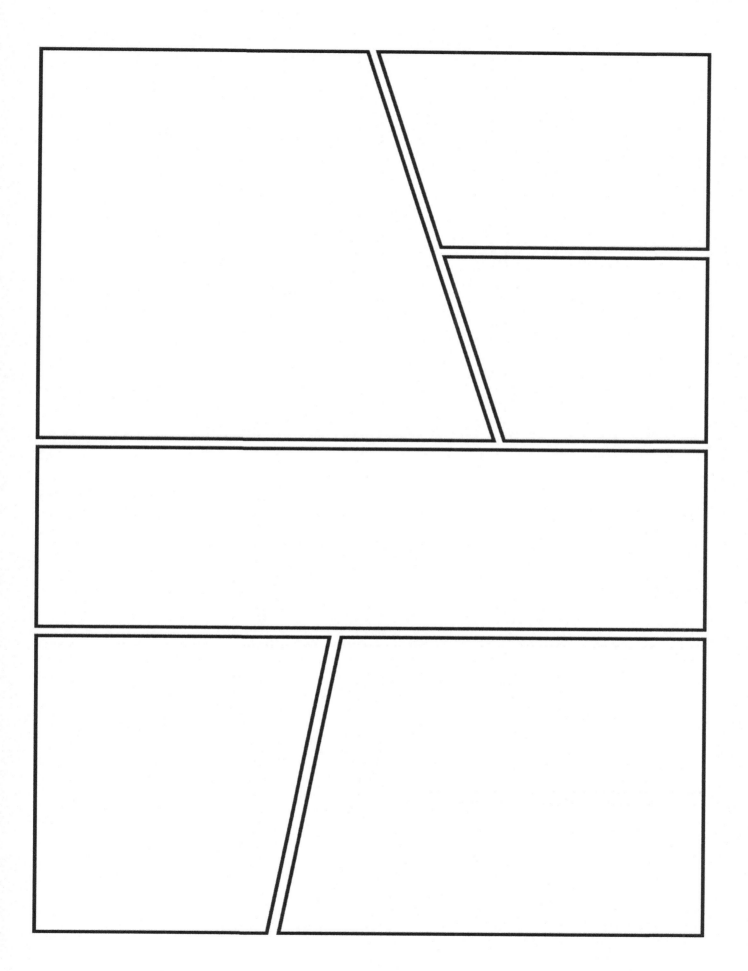